Fuel and Ovalhouse present

THE
DARK

WRITTEN BY NICK MAKOHA
DIRECTED BY ROY ALEXANDER WEISE

The Dark was first performed on 9th November 2018 at Tobacco Factory Theatres, Bristol and from 21st November to 1st December at Ovalhouse, London. Original team includes:

Roy Alexander Weise // **Director**
Michael Balogun // **Actor**
Akiya Henry // **Actor**
Rajha Shakiry // **Designer**
Neill Brinkworth // **Lighting Designer**
Duramaney Kamara // **Sound Designer**
Tanya Stephenson // **Production Stage Manager**
Jennifer Jackson // **Movement Director**
Joel Trill // **Voice Coach**
Lotte Hines // **Casting Director**

Co-commissioned by Fuel and Ovalhouse, supported by Arts Council England, The Cockayne Trust, The London Community Foundation, The Garrick Charitable Trust, Unity Theatre Trust and Sylvia Waddilove Foundation. Development supported by PULSE Festival, Coombe Farm Studios and as part of Ovalhouse's FiRST BiTES series.

·fuel

The Dark is produced by Fuel. Fuel produces an adventurous, playful and significant programme of work - live, digital, and across art forms – for a large and representative audience across the UK and beyond. We collaborate with outstanding artists with fresh perspectives and approaches who seek to explore our place in the world, expose our fears, understand our hopes for the future, create experiences which change us and in turn empower us to make change in the world. Fuel was founded in 2004 and is led by Kate McGrath.

Fuel's recent projects include: *Barber Shop Chronicles* (Inua Ellams), *Touching The Void* (David Greig), *Lock Her Up* (Fuel, University of Warwick and various artists), *Charlie Ward* (Sound&Fury), *So Many Reasons* (Racheal Ofori), *This Restless State* (Jesse Fox), *The Hartlepool Monkey* (Gyre and Gimble), *Dead Club* (Requardt & Rosenberg) and *An Evening with An Immigrant* (Inua Ellams).

The Fuel team is: Sarah Arden, Sabrina Begum, Hugo Chiarella, Daisy Drury, Grace Duggan, Mimi Findlay, Hattie Gregory, Sylvia Harrison, Stuart Heyes, Greg Howe, Che-Min Hsieh, David Lewis, Ella McCarthy, Kate McGrath, Molly Sharpe, Kirstin Shirling, Ines Tercio, Anna Williams, Sarah Wilson-White and Emilie Wiseman.

Fuel's trustees are: Sean Egan, Joe Hallgarten, Lilli Geissendorfer, Sue Hoyle and Shail Thaker.

Fuel is an Arts Council England National Portfolio Organisation.

"One of the most exciting and indispensable producing outfits working in British theatre today." **The Guardian**

"The maverick producing organisation who are prepared to invest in adventurous artists." **The Herald**

fueltheatre.com
@fueltheatre
#TheDark

Registered Charity No: 1149680
Registered as a company limited by guarantee in England: 7935786

OVALHOUSE

For the past 50 years Ovalhouse has been a home to experimental, radical and overlooked artists seeking to make theatre and performance that speaks to a world beyond the mainstream.

A hotbed of artistic activism in the five decades since we began, Ovalhouse has seen the social and artistic ideals it has aspired to become widely accepted as the model for a better society. We have sheltered social and political movements staffed by the stage and screen stars of the future, whilst pursuing an unerring agenda for positive artistic, political and social change. Ovalhouse stands on a proud history and continues to be a vital home for boundary-pushing art and artists with an eye on the future. With a theatre programme in two spaces we commission, co-produce and programme innovative work by early career and established artists, while our participation department provides a full range of programmes from inclusion projects to youth leadership training to supporting young artists. We invest in exploration and development, providing a space where artists can develop their creative practice, audiences can encounter new work and see the beginnings of new talent, and young people can use the arts to look at their lives, and develop their creativity and skills.

ovalhouse.com

Associate Artists
Bella Heesom
Dominique Le Gendre
Donnacadh O'Briain
Jesse Briton
Koko Brown
Yolanda Mercy

Young Associates
Amina Koroma
Emmanuel Simon
Helena Morais
Saffia Kavaz
Sera Mustafa
Tyrell Williams

Ovalhouse Staff List

Director
Deborah Bestwick

Executive Producer
Stella Kanu

General Manager
Gary Johnson

Head of Theatre and Artist Development
Owen Calvert-Lyons

Head of Communications and Audience Development
Monique Baptiste-Brown

Development Director
Katie Milton

Operations Manager
Alex Clarke

Technical Manager
Ina Berggren

Finance Manager
Yaw Manu

Buildings' Project Manager
Annika Brown

Learning and Participation Manager
Titilola Dawudu

Trusts and Foundations Manager
John Peterson

Demonstrate Project Manager
Elena Molinaro

Finance Assistant
Kwame T B Antwi

Producing Coordinator
Will Bourdillon

Press and Digital Marketing Officer
Sophie London

House Managers
Lily Batikyan
Steph Prior
James York

This is for my wife and children,
who make wherever I am with them home.
And to my mother, thank you for taking the risks you did
to give me the life I have.

A special thanks to Roy Alexander Weise.
You have become more than a director. Your passion is infectious.
I am proud to call you friend, confidant and ally.

Nick Makoha

THE DARK

A play in one act

OBERON BOOKS
LONDON

WWW.OBERONBOOKS.COM

First published in 2018 by Oberon Books Ltd
521 Caledonian Road, London N7 9RH
Tel: +44 (0) 20 7607 3637 / Fax: +44 (0) 20 7607 3629
e-mail: info@oberonbooks.com
www.oberonbooks.com

PB ISBN: 9781786827036
E ISBN: 9781786827043

Cover image: Carolyn Hill of ChillCreate

Printed and bound by Marston Book Services, Didcot.
eBook conversion by Lapiz Digital Services, India.

10 9 8 7 6 5 4 3 2 1

THE PLACE

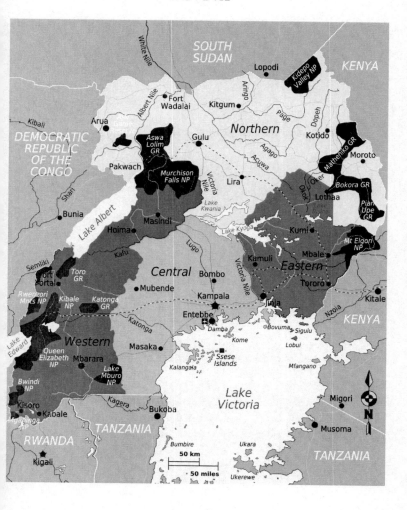

Characters

(in the order we meet them)

NARRATOR
Nick in present day.

YOUNG NICK
Four years old, lives with his father in Kampala.

MAMA NICK
Thirty-year-old PhD student living in London.
She has just returned to rescue her son.

JOYCE
Twenty-five-year-old Makarere University teacher.
Became a rebel because the Government killed her father.

OCHENG
Twenty-seven-year old Muslim matatu conductor, single.
Believes in Amin's Republic and democracy.

KIMATHI
Thirty-two. Matatu driver who smuggles goods from the border.

FATIMA
Twenty-two-year-old agriculture student returning home at the request of
her father. Leaving secret boyfriend back in Kampala. Preferred when the
colonials were here. Doesn't believe in rebels, afraid to show her faith.

MR FAIRFAX
Thirty-four-year-old expat English reporter.

OLD MAN
Seventy-four-year-old Ugandan.

MIREMBE

Twenty-eight-year-old hawker. Pregnant with fourth child.
Wants her own plot of land. Had two miscarriages.

KIGO

Mirembe's partner, thirty-four years old,
self-taught unemployed builder. Likes drinking and fishing.

SERGEANT 853

Thirty-eight-year-old Research Bureau officer with ambitions to rule.
Has a mistress and gambling habit.

OUMA

Eleven-year-old boy soldier. At five his Christian parents
were massacred and he became a street urchin.

SHOPKEEPER

Fifty-five-year-old man.

OPIO

Twenty-nine-year-old man. Joyce's husband.

CUSTOMS OFFICER

Forty-four-year-old white man.

CHARACTER NOTES:

The Dark is a two-character play where the actors
also play other characters. The opening section
is a prologue that leads them to the old Uganda Bus
Terminal in Kampala. Throughout the play
there is a sense of the supernatural/otherness.

'Nothing beautiful without struggle'

Plato, The Republic

'No Light, But Rather Darkness Visible'

John Milton, Paradise Lost

PROLOGUE

//Heathrow Airport, November 1979 – Night.

//MAMA NICK and YOUNG NICK stand at the back of the stage holding suitcases. MAMA NICK has a Ugandan passport in her hand. The audience enters from the side. Every so often MAMA NICK and YOUNG NICK move forward in the queue as the airport lights get brighter. Once the audience is settled we hear voices in the background. YOUNG NICK has been asked, 'Why are you here?' This is not heard by the audience. Airport background noises, not specific.

YOUNG NICK: Mama, where are we going?

MAMA NICK: Shh!

YOUNG NICK: But Mama?

MAMA NICK: Can you just?

CUSTOMS OFFICER: Mrs Akello! Can you come through please?

NARRATOR NICK: Hi, how was your journey? You could be anywhere in the world but your journey brought you here. Thanks for coming. I'm Nick…and I want to tell you a story. My story. My Journey. Stories are so important. They are fragments of memory and imagination that help us find out who we are and how we got to where we are. It is what separates us from The Dark. Sorry, that's a bit deep to start with. Well…you knew it wasn't gonna be a rom-com, youknowwhatImean, so… Anyways…I want you to do me a favour. I want you to close your eyes. You are me! The Nile is sleeping, a bus is waiting on the escarpment. The runway is tired. The trees, the earth, the sky have become houses for the dead. Bodies are skinned trees. Vehicles have no number plates houses have no doors. What name do you give me? Am I made of clouds, or of feathers? The air's murmurings, see how it argues with the sky? Night is not the only darkness. It keeps pouring onto the landscape. In this liquid heat the guards ignore you, and there are the watchmen, playing cards, drinking gin, eating banana figs. A girl my age is a ghost. My uncle has thrown his life in the lake. Is ghost another word for stranger? I have the eyes of a bird. The strangers are asking me to join them. Prisoners bring news. *If a stranger or anyone you do not know offers you the song, sing of everywhere.* On the edge of every day, an unnamed mountain sleeps.

//Projection: Uganda, 1979.

//We hear the sounds of Uganda/world-setting soundscape, which might include: mentions of the OPEC oil crisis, music playing, a weather forecast, and the sounds of gunfire.

REBEL BROADCAST: *(V/O – JOYCE's voice.)* I am here as a soldier. We are not on the battlefield but its shadow has followed us. Long live Uganda! People, ancestors and you not yet born, this is a day to remember. Attainment of nationhood. One year ago on this very site, a British flag was lowered and Uganda flag was raised. I have reached every corner of our nation in the last eight months. I cannot pretend that the Guerrillas are not trying to kill innocent citizens. Uganda, they talk about education, money that you will never see, of immunizations but not of freedom.

RADIO UGANDA: *(V/O.)* I, your servant, greet you, Uganda. My friends, my brothers you are in my heart. Your suffering is my suffering; we bled together in the cells or in battle. I will do my best to bring food back to our table and money back into our pockets. *(Applause.)* Our country is now in our hands. As the world watches, let us let go of our tribal feuds. Citizens, with your permission, I will watch over the republic. If foreigners act in any way that is contrary to our ways I will be swift to expel them. Countrymen, put down your guns and bayonets, as this will be a rule of peace. Uganda, the true Pearl of Africa, deserves it. Madams you will see me in your towns, cities, shanties and villages. Long live the Republic. *(Applause.)*

REBEL BROADCAST: *(V/O – JOYCE's voice.)* To the silent avengers! We are the refuge to the oppressed, the afflicted. We persecute our enemies who lie in wait like a lion, returning them to the dark that made them. Brace yourself in the savannahs, lakes, hills and rainforests. Shepherds sing your calling and I will come to you. We will be the voice of the wind and rain. Search for us in the night.

RADIO UGANDA: *(V/O.) It is believed that the former Vice President of Uganda who fled to neighbouring Tanzania after an alleged car crash on the Kampala-Jinja highway. He is gathering troops at the Tanzanian border. Also three soldiers and a farmer have been reported dead*

SCENE 1

//Old Taxi Park. During the scene it gets darker. MAMA NICK and YOUNG NICK are not yet on the bus. NARRATOR and YOUNG NICK are played by the same actor. NARRATOR is NICK now, grown up.

//Projection: Kampala, November 1979 – Dusk.

MIREMBE: Biscuit! Biscuit! Biscuit! The greatest Ugandan service a woman can perform is to spend her fertile years pregnant. When the skirt was illegal, they tried to wipe us out with machetes. But I multiply to defy our enemies. They will look you in the face to see if you are one of us until you are not. I sell them biscuits for ten shillings. From the profits I buy another package for two hundred and fifty shillings. If I'm lucky I go shopping. I saw this hat from a Bruce Lee film – *Fist of Fury.* As your father Kigo would say, 'When the rider is not welcome kick like a mule.' You will be my last of seven. I can take you as far as the border. Remember me? There is no such thing as the place you came from, there is only home. Soon my child like the birds you will be free.

OCHENG: Give me a pack.

MIREMBE: Just one?

OCHENG: Make it two. We are leaving soon. Be at the stage before curfew.

MIREMBE: But my customers!

OCHENG: So what!

//OCHENG walks to the side of the stage. He is talking to KIMATHI.

OCHENG: …I make two deliveries. The first in Jinja, to make sure it works. Then we do the border.

KIMATHI: Apana! We will not be able to get near to it. We will be exposed to bandits and drunk soldiers.

OCHENG: You don't have to. You have me and I will find someone else to pick it up. Rule number one brother, you always send someone else.

KIMATHI: I like that rule.

OCHENG: Listen! Even if that someone is stopped in Jinja they will only be getting a tenth of the product. Not from me. I'm the conductor. From someone else!

KIMATHI: Do you have someone in mind?

OCHENG: A woman.

KIMATHI: A woman? The biscuit lady!

OCHENG: No! I take her to Busia at least once a week. We need two peoples.

KIMATHI: A woman and a boy. *(Looking at NICK and MAMA NICK.)*

OCHENG: That is the plan.

KIMATHI: My plan.

OCHENG: My matatu gets your money to the border.

KIMATHI: We're in this together.

OCHENG: Partners.

KIMATHI: Partners.

OCHENG: *(Conductor.)* Pesa! Pesa! Pesa! Excuse me! Excuse me! Excuse me! My friends, please, unless you want the soldiers to arrange our fate, please pay attention to my instruction. I am the king of this matatu. Her name is Mable. Mable will get you to the border and our driver Kimathi has kindly sponsored us with half a tank of US petroleum which will get us as far as Jinja but as we know, oil is gold, so as you are boarding, please place your luggage under the seats. Yes! Four or five to a row...you sir, please make space for the lady?

OLD MAN: *(Getting onto the bus, humming.)* Is this seat taken/ Thank you sir.

I will be coming through for fares. Five hundred shillings to Namataba, one thousand shillings to Jinja and two thousand to Busia town. I have no change so exact fare and tips are welcome. Please do not forget the two hundred shillings petrol tax. Mable is thirsty. And be informed any bribes at checkpoints are your responsibility.

FAIRFAX: Pardon me I think your bag is on my foot?

As comrades in my principality, we offer you the many hills, the Mabira Forest, Njeru market and the Lake. Mable will be leaving in ten minutes. I am Ocheng, your conductor. Thank you! Thank you! Yes please! Yes please!

FATIMA: Assalam Alaikum sister how many months are you?

NARRATOR NICK: How you doing? On the bus so far is an old man, hunched with a wooden cane, maybe late seventies. I'm sure he had a glass eye. In front of him is a pretty young-ish lady, maybe early twenties, with a headscarf on. She carries a bag and some books in her arms. The Muzungu from England is the only white guy on the bus. He is clutching a camera and Dictaphone. Oh and that's the biscuit lady, she gets this bus regularly to pick up her stock. She is carrying a bun in the oven. Uganda's matatu service was not your usual bus service, no business cards, no union, no contracts, no insurance, no standard working hours, but if you wanted a simple way to get from point A to point B with no questions asked, then a matatu was your best bet.

OCHENG: Excuse me sir, no goats. Do I look like a shepherd to you? No guns. Sir, you had better put that camera away otherwise you and the whole bus will be deported.

//MAMA NICK and her son stand, holding a suitcase. Light is disappearing from the day. We hear the engine turn on and see the matatu lights coming on.

MAMA NICK: Nick kuja. Tuck your shirt in.

YOUNG NICK: Mama, where are we going?

NARRATOR NICK: That's Mama Nick. My mum. I hadn't seen her in a while because she'd been in London doing her PhD. She's the kind of woman who likes to keep herself to herself.

MAMA NICK: Two for Busia!

YOUNG NICK: Are we going to see Grandma? Are we Mama? Are we?

MAMA NICK: Yes! Yes! Grandma!

YOUNG NICK: Does she know we are coming?

YOUNG NICK: And Grandpa?

MAMA NICK: Yes! And Grandpa. *(To OCHENG.)* I need two for Busia, I'll pay you double.

Beat. The engine purrs.

OCHENG: You and you out!

FATIMA: But they paid.

OCHENG: I'm a capitalist.

FAIRFAX: Do you mind?

OCHENG: *(To existing customer.)* Pole! Pole sana.

MIREMBE: Yes Muzungu!! We all mind.

OCHENG: Everybody! Busia! Busia!

OLD MAN: Are you going to Gulu?

OCHENG: We are leaving now mama. It is almost curfew.

MIREMBE: Driver, will we be stopping for breaks?

OCHENG: We are not on safari.

MIREMBE: I'm going to be sick.

FATIMA: *(To MIREMBE.)* Have some peanuts?

MIREMBE: I would but since *(rubbing pregnant belly)* this one I can't stand them.

FATIMA: Try porridge. Is this your first? *(MIREMBE shakes her head.)*

MAMA NICK: Just sit down here and wait for mummy?

YOUNG NICK: Yes Mama.

//Projection (if needed): Uganda, November 1979 – Night.

//FAIRFAX speaks into a Dictaphone concealed in his top left breast pocket. He has a fever and a wound he is trying hard to conceal. He pauses on occasion to hear the news from the radio.

RADIO: *(V/O.)* The Ministry of Defence have appealed to the police security officer to cooperate with military police. We need to pull up our socks and systematically check who is going in and out of the country. We are still open for business.

FAIRFAX: They seem happy. How do they do it?

//Flashback. Outside Makenke Army Barracks, three days earlier.

FAIRFAX: Did anyone see you?

CAMERAWOMAN: No. *(She looks through camera lens.)*

FAIRFAX: How many graves?

CAMERAWOMAN: Five.

FAIRFAX: How many bodies?

CAMERAWOMAN: I'm not sure.

FAIRFAX: Show me?

CAMERAWOMAN: We have been spotted.

FAIRFAX: Let's split up. Get to the embassy. If I don't hear from you in three days, head for the border. Tanzania or Kenya. *(Gunshot.)*

Put us on a Routemaster near Carnaby Street and the expression would be the same.

MIREMBE: We are nothing like you.

OLD MAN: To you a worldly man as yourself, the metropolis must feel provincial. We must occur as savages. But tell me, in your country, do men still put on trousers one leg at a time? And when they shit, whether sitting or squatting, does it still come out of their arse?

MIREMBE: *(Chups.)* Idiot! Driver, go faster before this baby arrives?

SCENE 2

//A flashback. Projection: Bugiri Village, Uganda 1978 – Dawn.

//KIGO is holding his young child MIREMBE stands next to him.

KIGO: We have not named him yet.

MIREMBE: *(To KIGO privately.)* Weh Kigo! *(To audience.)* We have six children. Make sure I am married before the seventh arrives *(Rubs belly and chups)*.

KIGO: Mirembe if it carries on like this we will have to feed them dust or bullets. You curse my livelihood; must you steal my pride too? *(To audience.)* The firing has stopped. Shots would light up the sky. Here – 'The torture of the grave is only known by the corpse.'

MIREMBE: Chinua Achebe!

KIGO: *(Chups, then to audience.)* Over that hill, where I go night fishing, you find bullets in the flesh. Our presidents are locusts. They eat money but we the people are hungry. There goes another truck... Pepsi Cola on the side but that's the army.

MIREMBE: Are they hiring?

KIGO: Ahh! No work in a war for a builder. Who wants a builder when the aim of the game is to tear things down?

MIREMBE: A soldier gets paid to hold a gun while you talk to the clouds. Must all the money in this house come from my hand? The next child must be a daughter – someone who can carry water, fetch firewood, and whose words are their actions.

KIGO: Next you will want me to thresh millet and roast fish!

MIREMBE: Can you wear some balls please Kigo?

KIGO: Ah ah! Where water is boss, land must obey.

MIREMBE: After all I have done for you. Do I not deserve new dresses, jewellery, a wedding, dancing girls? Will you not even marry me and die so I can have something to show to my next husband? You can't even last till sunset without sleeping. When you look at yourself in the river does it even show you a man? *(Chups!)*

//Enter SERGEANT 853.

SERGEANT 853: Is she yours? You have caught a tiger. I like tigers. Get me some water! No, not you! Shine my shoes since you are down there. Tiger come! Tell her to

come! I would hate for you to have an accident. I am
a slow drinker. Do not hide on my account? And what
is the name of this cub? Tiger, let us not keep you from
your duties. Get up off your feet. Let me see your hands?
Hold that in your palm and let off a few rounds. Hmm!
Kalashnikov. Never breaks, jams or overheats. I can
offer you forty dollars a month, boots fatigues, bullets, a
bike, keys to a tank and I can't remember the last time I
paid for petrol. I only have two rules – find a way to last
the month – and I give the orders. We are leaving in ten
minutes. The choice is yours.

SCENE 3

//Later the same night as Scene 1, inside the matatu.

//Projection (if needed): Uganda, November 1979 – Night.

YOUNG NICK: Mama's eyes are staring at the rainforest. The
world is moving from left to right. *(Beat.)* My eyes are
dizzy. I can hear the drum of her heart, it is loud and fast.
It is eight p.m. Mama has not yet told me to go to sleep.
Wow! Baba would never allow this. *(Giggling.)*

//Flashback: Earlier, Kampala golf club – Day.

BABA NICK: Bend the knees.

YOUNG NICK: Like this Baba?

BABA NICK: No like this.

YOUNG NICK: The golf club is heavy Baba.

BABA NICK: Have a go?

YOUNG NICK: I did it Baba!

BABA NICK: Hehe! You did my son. You did.

YOUNG NICK: The driver is swerving to avoid potholes. Only
the old man in the corner is asleep peacefully. I count cars
as the driver turns the radio up.

RADIO: *(V/O.)* A new law: women cannot wear trousers.
Kalule will be fighting Ray Seales and a boy is missing
from Kampala, last seen with his father at the golf club.

//Later the same night as Scene 1, inside the matatu.

NARRATOR NICK: My mother offers kikoys to all the ladies
in exchange for silence. A woman wearing trousers offers
dried fish and another chapatti. We share what we have
of soda. We eat in silence with our hands once the elder
(now awake) has blessed the food. We use water from
the jerrycan to wash our hands out the window. The
conductor Ocheng hands the driver his portion. He takes
mouthfuls on the straights. The women wrap their kikoys
around their waists.

FATIMA: You are right. On this bus, can anyone really sleep?
(Eats while staring at the boy.)

MIREMBE: My back! *(Rubbing her pregnant belly.)*

FATIMA: I am sleeping on the right side of my face. *(Tilts her
head in pain.)*

MIREMBE: The old man snores. If it is not dogs barking, then
it is the sky. What kind of rain is this? It smells like blood.
(To FAIRFAX.) Do you mind Muzungu, your elbow?

FATIMA: *(Hushed tones.)* The woman and the boy! You know her?

MIREMBE: No! She speaks like the Queen of England.

FATIMA: Hmmm! She must be a so-and-so.

MIREMBE: Look at the kikoy she gave me. Expensive!

FATIMA: And she bought the whole row of seats for herself.

MIREMBE: All!

FATIMA: She has my vote. I hear in England you can never get malaria!

MIREMBE: Yah and their trains go underground. Does she know Amin?

FATIMA: Who?

MIREMBE: The Queen? I mean is she in the government?

FATIMA: When can you depend on them for anything?

MIREMBE: Who can we blame?

FATIMA: If you know what is good for you, you will blame no one. I have the wrong name, you have the wrong face and you are pregnant. So Nyamaza unless you want to end up like the president's wife...

MIREMBE: Cut like chicken for all to see on television...

FATIMA: I was in my dorms when they...

MIREMBE: ...No state funeral, just some picture in a paper. It was the boyfriend?

FATIMA: The doctor? Tell me why a doctor kills the woman he loves? Does a president with five wives and who knows how many mistresses, need to kill his wife?

MIREMBE: Maybe The Queen is his mistress?

FATIMA: Her! *(Looking at MAMA NICK.)* She could pass for a mistress.

MIREMBE: Women die when soldiers have our body on their mind.

FATIMA: They should be minding their business.

MIREMBE: You are their business. Whether you are carrying water from the well, food from the market, a sibling in your arms. My brother was a houseboy for one of the generals back in Kampala. He says it was one of the soldiers. They fight like wildebeest, fuck like teenagers. Said he had his eye on Kay. That he was her bodyguard. A husband must tend to his cattle. If he doesn't then well...let's just say that the soldier was a fox dancing around the hen house.

FATIMA: I am not cattle!

MIREMBA: We are all cattle. You just do not know who is your cowboy.

SCENE 4

//Projection: By a Checkpoint outside Jinja, November 1979 – Night. One hour earlier.

//Two SOLDIERS at a checkpoint. One is reading a newspaper, the other is looking into the night.

SOLDIER 1: What is it, Kigo? *(SOLDIER 1 turns a page.)*

Long beat.

KIGO: Nothing! Do you know the Vice President?

SOLDIER 1: Should I?

KIGO: He has gone. *(SOLDIER 1 slaps a mosquito off his neck.)*

SOLDIER 1: Good for him. Then there will be more for us. Now shut up so I can read my paper?

KIGO: He is one of us.

SOLDIER 1: Are his pockets filled with nothing?

KIGO: No.

SOLDIER 1: We stand in the road so that he can fill his pockets. Looking at nothing.

KIGO: But it is beautiful.

SOLDIER 1: Between grief and nothing I choose grief. How about you?

KIGO: Do you have anything to drink?

SOLDIER 1: You had the last of it.

KIGO: I choose nothing.

SOLDIER 1: Over grief?

KIGO: Yes!

SOLDIER 1: We already have that, Kigo. *(SOLDIER 1 looks up from his paper.)*

   Beat.

KIGO: If I can't have it all I would rather have nothing.

SOLDIER 1: Soldier I have no TV, or wife telling me all her thoughts. I only have this paper to entertain me. Now unless what you have to say is better than these lies and half-truths, then your time for words is up. Let your eyes find sleep

KIGO: I'm heading to Busia on my next shift. Sergeant 853 says he needs me on the frontline. I hear the Tanzanians are coming in that way.

SOLDIER 1: Well good luck to you, Kigo.

   //SOLDIER 1 goes back to his paper. KIGO slaps a mosquito that has landed on his face or neck.

SCENE 5

//Projection: By a river outside Jinja, November 1979 – Night.

YOUNG NICK: Mama! I can't sleep

MAMA NICK: Mandazi?

YOUNG NICK: No Mama, Thank you. It hurts when I close my eyes.

MAMA NICK: Do you want some water?

YOUNG NICK: Emem. *(Shaking head.)*

MAMA NICK: *(Strokes his hair and sings.)*

Beat.

YOUNG NICK: What are you singing?

MAMA NICK: Shhh! Sleep, sleep little one.

YOUNG NICK: I haven't prayed mama.

MAMA NICK: OK, close your eyes? Dear God…

YOUNG NICK: Dear God!

MAMA NICK: Thank you for this day, thank you for my son, thank you for our new friends and for keeping us safe in this bus.

YOUNG NICK: Dear God. Thank you God for mama and baba and grandma and grandpa. I love mama and I love you God, I love you forever and I love you like the sun.

BOTH: Amen!

//The conductor tunes the radio to a rebel broadcast.

//Rebel Broadcast, near a river outside Jinja.

JOYCE: *(She is crouching, face smeared with red paint. Gunshots in the distance.)* When we were hungry, where were the mediums, shaman, tribal elders, gurus, renowned teachers? Women you of the ordinary life; you of the common day, you with sons and pregnant bellies, you who tend to cattle, tend to men, tend to the land and its needs. Hear me! They call our bodies weak but was it not our wombs that bore them a nation? We have the heart of kings, so test your mettle and join me. On the pulse of this night I will call on you my sisters to join me in arms. So before they erase the story of the mother, the woman, the child and our people, let us send a message and build us a future parallel to this one where our women can be mothers, wives and sisters again! Look me in the eye and tell me we are not our own stories. I am sick of this illusion, manifest as war. A person must know oneself in their own head. Are they cast to endure or are they cast to turn and run? War is a house in the middle of the ocean, a house of dampness, a house of burning, a house of...

OPIO: Joyce! Joyce!

//JOYCE wipes the paint off her face, picks up the firewood and returns to her homestead.

YOUNG NICK: Mama!

MAMA NICK: Go back to sleep!

YOUNG NICK: *(To audience.)* The journey to Busia, my grandparents' home, means we won't be back to Kampala by morning. I never got to say bye to my dad. Mama promised Baba she would have me back by morning so that he can drive me to the school in his Datsun.

//Flashback: Kampala, Baba Nick's sitting room.

27

//BABA NICK sings:

London Bridge is falling down,
Falling down, falling down,
London Bridge is falling down,
My fair Lady.

Build it up with wood and clay,
Wood and clay, wood and clay,
Build it up with wood and clay,
My fair Lady.

SCENE 6

//Later, the same night as Scene 1, inside the matatu.

//The OLD MAN is singing.

OLD MAN: Who are you running back to?

FATIMA: Pardon.

OLD MAN: You keep looking at the road behind us.

FATIMA: I am not you, Muzee.

OLD MAN: If you keep running you will be. As the trees get smaller the heart burns.

FATIMA: My heart is not on fire, Muzee.

OLD MAN: Then what are you running from?

FATIMA: No one. Answer your own questions, Muzee.

OLD MAN: A chief does not answer his own questions

FATIMA: You are Chief? With what kingdom?

OLD MAN: Because you cannot see my people you cannot see the king.

FATIMA: A king. You sound like my father. He thinks he owns the whole Jinga. Insha'Allah one day he will.

OLD MAN: So that is who you are running to. But who are you running from?

FATIMA: No one.

OLD MAN: My first wife used to say you must be in a position to give your wives all the hospitality they want.

FATIMA: Do you know what women want?

OLD MAN: Ask your husband.

FATIMA: He is not my husband...yet.

OLD MAN: Lucky you.

FATIMA: *(Laughs.)* I don't even know his face. *(Beat.)*

OLD MAN: I am on a bus after curfew heading for the border.

FATIMA: So where are you running to?

OLD MAN: *(Laughing.)*

SCENE 7

REBEL BROADCAST: *Fear not, Uganda, our brothers and sisters in exile are coming for us. We are not stone but a river moving in all directions. You too must be like water and join us.*

//In the matatu, later that night.

YOUNG NICK: Mama I need to pee.

FAIRFAX: Do we have to stop again?

FATIMA: Don't you have children?

FAIRFAX: Excuse me.

FATIMA: Or a bladder?

FAIRFAX: How very dare you?

OCHENG: Mama I'm stopping.

MAMA NICK: Thank you. But the Muzungu *(To FAIRFAX)* will pee in a cup.

FAIRFAX: *(He rewinds and replays fragments of dialogue from his Dictaphone.)* Does it bother you that we are going round and round in circles? *(He rewinds the tape.)* The bodies. *(He rewinds the tape then forwards it.)* Does it bother you that we are going round and round in circles?

(Stops tap and starts recording into Dictaphone.) The President is seeking international support in reinforcing his army and air force. It is believed that his predecessor has Acholi and Langi soldiers who have infiltrated the barracks across the country with the intention of handing power to the old

regime. One such attempt was thwarted. *(He rewinds the tape and presses play.)*

(He forwards the tape to continue recording.) We were not able to corroborate this but we were able to capture a sighting of a grave being dug and soldiers being dumped in their uniforms face to foot. This testimony bears little weight without the photographic evidence. I can only hope that Nell has made it out alive. I will inform the British Consulate in Nairobi. The airport is not safe for extraction.

KIMATHI: Who are you talking to?

FAIRFAX: Erm. I do have children.

OCHENG: Good for you.

FAIRFAX: Two of them. Eliza and John.

OCHENG: I once had a girlfriend called Eliza.

FAIRFAX: I hope it wasn't my daughter. *(Laughter.)*

OCHENG: What?

FAIRFAX: I jest.

OCHENG: No it wasn't your daughter.

FAIRFAX: I know.

OCHENG: She was a Langi girl. I don't think your daughter is Langi.

FAIRFAX: No it was a joke.

OCHENG: *(Beat.)* That's a strange joke.

FAIRFAX: Yes, I know.

Beat.

OCHENG: So why are you not looking after them?

FAIRFAX: I've been working here. I'll be home soon. I've just got to meet a colleague first. We need to get a shot of the crook in action. The money shot.

OCHENG: Okay.

FAIRFAX: I haven't spoken to them in weeks.

OCHENG: Do they write to you?

FAIRFAX: No. Sometimes.

OCHENG: Bet you can't wait to see them.

FAIRFAX: Yes. John will be so thrilled and fascinated to see my gunshot wound.

OCHENG: Wound?

//FAIRFAX shows it.

OCHENG: I have some waragi if you want to clean it.

FAIRFAX: No. I'll wait till I get to a hospital, thanks.

OCHENG: You Muzungus are crazy.

FAIRFAX: Why?

OCHENG: Perfectly normal life at home in England and you are here.

FAIRFAX: I want to do something with my life. Help, maybe?

OCHENG: Who are your cassettes helping? Not me. Nor anyone on this bus.

YOUNG NICK: Some of the passengers to pee in the bush. Mama keeps me close to the matatu and tells the driver to keep the engine running. She lets me pee by the wheel arch of the rear tire, then she goes after me. Four left for the bushes but five return. Four with their hands up one with a gun. The one with a gun is a boy, maybe a head taller than me.

//Back to outside the matatu, later the same night.

//YOUNG NICK and MAMA NICK can see this from the matatu. Passengers are peeing in the bush as OUMA arms his gun. He grabs one by the throat.

FATIMA: Can we not pee in peace?

OUMA: Shut up! *(Pointing gun at them.)*

OLD MAN: Boy leave them, they are not soldiers.

OUMA: Shut up, old man. Do you call someone with a gun boy? *(Waving his gun.)*

OLD MAN: Point it at me! These women could be your mothers.

Boy in army fatigues has his palm
on a gun. Boy smokes ganja,
says it makes him run.
Boy leads a battalion but can't spell
his name. Boy has river of AIDS
running through his veins.

FAIRFAX: I have money, give me the gun?

OUMA: I can't. This gun killed my mother! Do you want to join her?

//Screams from women.

OLD MAN: *(To the women.)* Nyamaza! *(To OUMA.)* Point the gun at me?

Boy sleeps with twelve virgins
to make it disappear. Bet you boy
will be Abraham by the end of the year!
Boy's back teeth as sharp
as bayonets. Sucks her breast
with war-gin breath.

OUMA: How much is there?

FAIRFAX: Two thousand shillings. *(Beat.)*

OUMA: *(Wiping his eyes.)* Baba, do you know what this buys?

OLD MAN: My freedom?

OUMA: Your life.

OLD MAN: I thought you didn't want money?

OUMA: I thought you wanted to live?

Boy thinks he's Chuck Norris,
thinks he's Bruce Lee. Boy learned
Krav Maga in training camps led by Israelis.

//Flashback – Projection: Forest, two hours earlier – Night.

//Sound of boy soldiers singing and marching. Ouma lets the troop march into the distance while he and an injured boy soldier lag behind.

OUMA: *Wait! (To the injured boy soldier.)* Sit down here and rest. *(Beat.)* You have done well brother.

//The injured boy's wounds are too severe. OUMA examines him then sits with him for a moment looking at the moon.

OUMA: Isn't it beautiful brother? The Moon. *(The wounded boy nods as they watch the moon.)*

Beat.

//OUMA twists his neck to put him out of his misery. OUMA holds him for a while in silence then leaves his body.

YOUNG NICK: The night is waiting for us. It does not move.

//MAMA rises from the ground.

OUMA: Mama, Mama is it you?

MAMA NICK: No boy!

OUMA: Mama, it is you? Take me with you. Give me a name. Give me wings. I am fed up with marching while we sleep and making home on the back of trees. Help me? Even lions and snakes roam free. This gun has known me since I was four. Teach me how to hold something else. Mama, hold me the way I used to hold a football.

MAMA NICK: What is your name boy!

OUMA: Ouma.

MAMA NICK: Come to me, Ouma.

NARRATOR NICK: Mama calls him over without blinking, as
if she is taming a lion. Mama keeps her mind even though
she is trembling. She reaches, with the length of her whole
body, for his gun with one hand, and hugs him with the
other. I hug him too. Mama pays his fare and hands him
some clothes she bought for children in our home village.
There is nothing to do but to keep on driving. Only the
boy is sleeping. Mama has his gun. The lines in the road
are blurring into one. So I watch the moon.

SCENE 8

//Projection (if needed): Rebel broadcast, Lake Victoria, November 1979.

//JOYCE is staring at the same moon over the lake, we can hear water.

JOYCE: *(Into mic.)* You iron men, what honour is there in
uniforms? Even a shear cropper can make himself worthy
in battle. Red dirt is a beautiful burial ground. When we
had no roof, was not the shamba our home? When we had
no eyes, did not the Nile listen? When we had no ears, did
not the hills surround us?

*//There is another with her; their faces are covered. They are drawing
a map in the dirt. When the plan is finished the comrade picks a
jerrycan of water, places it on her head and heads back towards
town to disguise her absence. JOYCE finishes her broadcast.*

JOYCE: *(Into mic.)* When we had no thoughts, did not our
mothers pull tilapia from the riverbed to feed our clans,
did not the sun comfort us by day and the moon by
night? Watch the birds navigate the air? Remember when
the hunt was our fortune? Like buffalo we must find our

foothold. In the quarrel of combat we emerge from the fields, farms and from behind the stove like a new spirit.

//The moon comes into vision. JOYCE stares at it as she scrubs out the dirt map. JOYCE is on her way back to Jinja with wood on her back.

SCENE 9

//We're back inside the matatu. An oncoming car flashes twice to signal for a checkpoint.

OUMA: Turn off the lights. Whatever you do, do not stop.

FAIRFAX: It is just a checkpoint.

OUMA: The lights. Take us back where you came.

FAIRFAX: On these roads, have you seen the potholes?

KIMATHI: Brother!

OCHENG: Stay calm.

KIMATHI: I'm calm.

//The matatu slows to a halt at the checkpoint.

SOLDIER: This is a private road, my friend, and it is past curfew. Do you have a permit?

OCHENG: Sorry boss.

SOLDIER: You know the rules, it is past curfew.

OCHENG: How much?

SOLDIER: Don't insult me, who is on the bus?

OCHENG: Villagers.

FATIMA: Who are you calling a villager?

SOLDIER: And the boys? All of you, out.

MAMA NICK: Is there a problem, officer?

SOLDIER: Is my business your business?

MAMA NICK: The boys are mine.

SOLDIER: Your names please?

MAMA NICK: Okello.

SOLDIER: Okello, and your sons' names?

MAMA NICK: Luke and John.

SOLDIER: Your disciples? Well hallelujah. Excellent!

Beat.

My friends will be taking this vehicle. Leave the passengers on the side with their possessions.

MAMA NICK: Officer!

SOLDIER: Yes madam.

MAMA NICK: We think you dropped this. *(MAMA hands him a bag of money.)*

SOLDIER: Yes madam I did. *(Counting the money.)*

MAMA NICK: Officer, can we go?

SOLDIER: Am I stopping you?

MAMA NICK: *(To audience.)* Those in charge are not fools.
They never die for their country. They teach others to
do that for them, men who would rather see the shirt off
our backs than see us alive. When we were young did we
not run in those fields and shoot finch with catapults?
(To OCHENG.) Whatever it is that you're doing, you'd
better bring it to a stop. Understand?

OCHENG: Yes, madam.

SCENE 10

//Inside the matatu, later the same night.

NARRATOR NICK: The world behind us keeps disappearing
into darkness. The headlights search for the road ahead
that snakes forward. The radio talks about the price of oil
when a *tire bursts.* The matatu moves right as our bodies
move left. The matatu is limping on its left side. A woman
is calling God's name in Arabic she has her arm around
the old man to stop him from falling. The biscuit lady tucks
herself into the corner of the matatu, her arms wrapped
around her swollen belly, while the driver curses in Swahili.

OCHENG: Mama we have to stop. We have a puncture.

MAMA NICK: Jinja is a not far? Take this? Can you get tyres?

OCHENG: I know a place.

MAMA NICK: Quickly!

39

OCHENG: Yes Mama.

FATIMA: Driver here is my fare, I can walk from here Insha'Allah.

OLD MAN: Is it safe young lady. *(Beat.)*

FATIMA: We shall see. *(Beat.)* Assalam Alaikum Muzee.

OLD MAN: Walaikum Assalam.

NARRATOR NICK: Fatima grabs her bags off the rack. Her hijab blowing in her face. She waves at the old man and winks at me. As she shouts her goodbyes the rest curse the driver. Only the old man and I see her leave. Not towards the town, but back where we came from.

SCENE 11

//Projection: Jinja, November 1979 – the same night.

OCHENG: Weh! How much for the tyres?

SHOPKEEPER: A thousand shillings. It is too late for the boy.

OCHENG: The boy stays! And some petrol?

SHOPKEEPER: Has your car broken down?

OCHENG: What storm would that be? Tell me, why is my life important to you?

SHOPKEEPER: I am just asking brother.

OCHENG: Brother! Are we friends?

SHOPKEEPER: I am not asking for trouble.

OCHENG: Will there be?

SHOPKEEPER: Be what?

OCHENG: Trouble?

SHOPKEEPER: Is there anything else?

OCHENG: No.

SHOPKEEPER: Have I done something wrong?

OCHENG: To who?

SHOPKEEPER: To you?

OCHENG: Is that what you are asking?

SHOPKEEPER: Well I need to close we are past curfew.

OCHENG: Curfew?

SHOPKEEPER: Yes.

OCHENG: What curfew?

SHOPKEEPER: Now!

OCHENG: Now is not a time.

SHOPKEEPER: At Dark!

OCHENG: When does it get Dark?

SHOPKEEPER: I don't want any trouble.

OCHENG: Do I look like trouble to you?

SHOPKEEPER: No!

OCHENG: Is this your shop?

SHOPKEEPER: My wife and I took it when the Indians left.

OCHENG: Close your eyes?

SHOPKEEPER: Why?

OCHENG: If you do not close your eyes there will be
trouble… Do you see it?

//The driver grabs a can of petrol.

SHOPKEEPER: Okay. What am I looking for?

OCHENG: Do you see it?

SHOPKEEPER: You mean the Dark? *(Beat.)*

OCHENG: Yes! *(OCHENG steels a tyre and beckons to YOUNG
NICK to come with him.)* Can you feel it?

SHOPKEEPER: Yes!

OCHENG: That is where we came from. *(They run. The
SHOPKEEPER opens his eyes.)*

NARRATOR NICK: A woman's voice who is not my mother
is talking in Samia to Ocheng from outside the store.
She carries water on her back.

JOYCE: Is that your matatu down the road?

OCHENG: Do I know you?

JOYCE: If you want to get where you are going before the
end of the night you better get off the main road, there
are soldiers in civilian dress before you enter. Let me in
and I will show you a better route.

OCHENG: We need petrol too. Mable is thirsty.

JOYCE: Follow me!

YOUNG NICK: The men push the matatu into the town, Jinja.
The new lady keeps looking at Mama's face. Does she
know her?

SCENE 12

//Jinja – later the same night.

*//The matatu is parked outside JOYCE's house by the servants' quarters
and a cooking hut.*

YOUNG NICK: Baba you want some water? We arrive to a
clearing of huts some of wood and some of stone with
mabati roofs. The woman called Joyce escorts us to the
cooking hut. She is pretty but she never smiles.

JOYCE: Give them some food and water.

YOUNG NICK: She takes the driver and Ocheng behind the
huts with no walls to the shamba.

JOYCE: You can take what you need from here.

YOUNG NICK: Joyce's eyes are on Ouma. Ouma looks to the floor. Mama's eyes are on the huts, some with lamps and others with men smoking in the shadows. Mama asks her…

MAMA NICK: How much for the petrol and food?

JOYCE: Are we not sisters?

MAMA NICK: How much?

JOYCE: A seat on the bus.

MAMA NICK: A seat on the bus.

JOYCE: I could use a woman like you.

MAMA NICK: You don't know a woman like me.

JOYCE: I know you want to be on the other side of the border.

MAMA NICK: Don't you?

JOYCE: This is our country.

MAMA NICK: Our country is falling apart.

JOYCE: Stay.

MAMA NICK: And fall apart with it?

JOYCE: Then fight.

MAMA NICK: I will leave that to the men.

JOYCE: They are falling apart.

MAMA NICK: I am not a politician.

JOYCE: We don't need politicians right now.

MAMA NICK: What do we need?

JOYCE: Warriors. *(Whispered.)* Look for me in the night.

MAMA NICK: If I become a warrior I lose the boy.

JOYCE: If we don't become warriors then we lose all our boys. Girls too.

MAMA NICK: I cannot feed my son on dust and bullets.

JOYCE: You think your purse can solve the problem?

MAMA NICK: When has bloodshed brought peace?

JOYCE: Peace will not get us what we want.

Beat.

JOYCE: Then give me your gun?

MAMA NICK: What gun?

JOYCE: Mama! You hold your purse tight but you offer your money freely. Give me the gun. Give me the gun since you are on your way out.

//Enter OPIO.

OPIO: Joyce, we must talk now.

JOYCE: Excuse me one minute, my husband is still awake… What is it?

OPIO: Must I spell it out?

JOYCE: Yes, I'm busy!

OPIO: What can be more busy than our marriage? Our house is standing there quiet, your classroom is empty, our bed is cold and the shamba vegetables are overripe.

JOYCE: I have still to wipe the blood from the loss of our second child and you are concerned about the warmth of a mattress.

OPIO: We both lost a child, and ignoring me will not make him return. This is the most you have said to me in a month. Must I wait for another set of strays to wander into our village before we finish what we have to say?

JOYCE: At least they see me when I talk. Your eyes do not even reach mine. Why don't you caress my belly, hold my bosoms or comb my hair in the evenings. Is it because my body is no longer filled with your child?

I must be cursed. You care for your motorbike more than you do me. You bathe her every day, feed her oil. Where do you take her first thing in the morning? Passed the mangroves and rail track? The scent of oil can't hide the smell of perfume. *(Beat.)* Now you see me.

OPIO: Did I rip this child from your belly? Was it me that returned him back to the earth? Are not my tears the same weight as yours? My very name on your tongue tastes of bark. You know sometimes I wake up to my blanket burning. Not form the heat of the night or my flesh but form the heat of my own thoughts. Forgive me! She meant nothing.

JOYCE: She meant something. Eight summers we have been married to each other. She meant something. Eight

rainy seasons we have ploughed these fields. She meant
something. Eight years I have held you in my heart and this
ring on my finger.

OPIO: Joyce!

JOYCE: When the driver is ready I will leave with them. Let go
of me! Whatever we have is yours. You no longer have to
hide your women in darkness.

OPIO: Joyce, if you fight for the rebels, you will die. *(Beat.)*
I'm sorry.

JOYCE: I have already died twice what can be worse? *(To MAMA
NICK.)* Mama the driver says we will ready to leave in ten
minutes. Once you have had enough to eat let us go!

OPIO: Joyce. *(To the audience.)*

JOYCE: Mama let us go. *(The matatu engine fires up.)*

NARRATOR NICK: Kimathi starts the engine and we all get into
the matatu. Joyce is last. She only carries a rucksack.

FAIRFAX: I hate to be an absolute toerag but this is my stop chaps.

OCHENG: As I said, follow the road to the right and you will see
the hotel on the left.

FAIRFAX: Did you happen to get any change for my fare?

OCHENG: Muzungu I told you exact fares only. Mable is thirsty.

//The sound of the matatu leaving Jinja.

OLD MAN/NARRATOR NICK: *(Humming.)* I used to eat hippo
meat at Kabalega Falls with the Muzungus every night until

I saw my neighbour floating among the crickets. Even the colonials do not want to stay.

Who were we before they came? Was there a time when we were alone among ourselves? Where is that story in your books?

OLD MAN: They left without even saying goodbye. Because I am old I am useless. I smell of paraffin, Waragi and cigarettes.

NARRATOR NICK: All I need is some place to sleep and food in belly before my time comes,

OLD MAN: Or when Time comes to get me.

SCENE 13

//Later that night in another street in Jinja. We hear footsteps walking down the street. A knock at the door. No answer. Another knock at the door, no answer. Then the door frames OPIO. Who he is speaking to is unseen. (YOUNG NICK is not in the scene.)

SERGEANT 853: It is you again, Opio. To what do we owe the pleasure?

OPIO: I have news.

Beat.

SERGEANT 853: A fish cannot walk by itself. Spit it out.

OPIO: The rebel broadcasts.

SERGEANT 853: Yes.

OPIO: I know their location. It is my wife.

SERGEANT 853: Very good. Come in.

OPIO: Sir.

SCENE 14

//Projection (if needed): Busia, Uganda, November 1979 – Night.

//Busia is the border town, and it is one and a half hours later the same night.

REBEL BROADCAST: *(V/O.)* Split the rock. It is that hour. We cannot wait another day. It is time to turn the machete into a sword, a matatu into a chariot. How else will the voice of freedom sing in our land again?

RADIO UGANDA *(V/O.)* A fatal accident following a head collision between a hyena and a Range Rover. A boy is still missing, last seen with a woman heading east. Also, the archbishop has not been seen for days.

YOUNG NICK: The smell of fish is strong in my hometown. Everyone knows Mama in Busia. There was an officer was waiting for her when we arrived. To avoid his vehicle being confiscated, Kimathi told them everything he knew. They were not interested in the boy soldier or the white man with nice trousers, they only wanted the woman with the new voice, the lady who sold biscuits and the lady who joined us at Jinja. She escaped through the back door of the Matatu and ran far far away. I hope they don't find her. How were we going to see grandma and fish with grandpa now?

SCENE 15

//Projection: Police Barrack Interior, Interrogation. Uganda, November 1979 – Night.

//INTERROGATION 1: A generator can be heard. The light in the interrogation room flickers on and off.

MIREMBE: Kigo? Kigongo? Please! I'm innocent, help me. The baby. Please Kigo. Tell them?

KIGO: Shut up.

MIREMBE: Kigo?

KIGO: Were my instructions not enough?

MIREMBE: We have no money Kigo!

KIGO: Say my name again and they will kill us both.

MIREMBE: No they can't.

KIGO: Shhh. *(KIGO hushes her.)* Where are the children?

MIREMBE: Kampala.

KIGO: With who? *(Beat.)* Mirembe? *(Knock at the door.)*

MIREMBE: Don't hurt me

KIGO: If I don't they will.

MIREMBE: The baby.

KIGO: I don't make the rules. I'm sorry. Shut up, shut up, shut up.

//The generator in the police barracks stops and we are in darkness.

//INTERROGATION 2: This interview is in darkness. MAMA NICK's purse is on the table. She reaches in for her money, counts it and hides it in her underwear. SERGEANT 853 enters.

SERGEANT 853: What a prize. *(Checking through MAMA NICK's bag with a lighter.)* Hmm! A bracelet, a watch, lipstick, passport. *(Looking through the passport.)* Akello! – A gun. *(To MAMA NICK.)* This is one of ours. – *(Beat.)* – Madame Akello! Your shenanigans have cut short my visit to State House. How are you feeling?

//MIREMBE's screams can be heard from next door.

Your friend really wants our attention? Shall we begin? Tell me what we need to hear and you can go free. You cannot be a mother while you are in here. Let's not waste time. Silence will not save you. I, like God, can offer you freedom. I hope you are not trying to rob us of our country. Is this how you repay us in paradise? We know you have met with a rebel sympathizer. And your son's father will be here by morning to return him back to Kampala. As well as your adopted son. Holy mother. Uganda's own Mother Theresa with a Muzungu accent.

MAMA NICK: I have nothing to say.

(In Samia.) Mwanna wefwe hasi ndi omusungu. Ndebulirwa hunno. Olukongo yi mama atula luri amwalo awo. Babba yali omunabi. Atta tebaho omundu yesi, anno bosi bamumanyire. Ndaheba endye omwana wange ni hutula hulukongo lulala nende latangene? Amachi sikeruhanga ohutula mumwalo. (My brother, I am not a Muzungu. I was born here. My mother's village is just down the road. My father was a fisherman. Ask anyone,

51

they will tell you about him. Why would I steal my own
child, when me and his father are from the same tribe?
Water does not run away from the river.)

Beat.

SERGEANT 853: Hasi nisio sihutebere. (Wrong answer.)
(Laughing and wiping hands with a handkerchief.) Make sure
there is money on the table when I come back. Forgive
me! Where are my manners? *(To KIGO.)* Get the lady a
drink, Kigo. And let the biscuit lady go.

//SERGEANT 853 exits.

SCENE 16

//Outside the Police Barracks in Busia, a little while later.

YOUNG NICK: Ouma and I sat on the steps of the barracks
not saying a word. I had always wanted a brother. He
kept looking into the night as if he could see into it, every
passing car got his attention. I still had the ball he had
given my mother. To pass the time we showed off our
skills. This was the first time I had seen him smile. Power
cuts shut the game down. In our game of light, the edges
of things were lost and borderless like the conversations
that began in a dream. I asked him where he was from
and he spoke with his hands, pointing into the forest. The
dust rose in the air as a jeep approached, Ouma's gaze
once again distracted. A man in uniform with the label
853 on his chest stepped out, closely followed by two
others. Ouma pulled me into the darkness and gestured
for me to stay there as he followed them like a ghost into
the barracks.

The generators had not yet turned on. With my body
pressed to the wall I could not see but I heard bodies fall
and a scream. Ouma returned with a gun strapped around
his waist. My mother follows, her face swollen. He jump-
starts the car and we head with my mother towards the
border. The headlights are off. The soldiers emerge from
the building. Sergeant 853 shooting into the sky, his men
shooting at us. I am not sure if they hit the petrol tank or
the tyres but the jeep stops yards before the crossing. We
jump out. Mirembe the biscuit lady falls to the floor. She
holds her belly and screams in pain. Mama picks her up,
hushes her and lifts her quickly from the ground. She is
covered in mud. Ouma scoops me up and motions for us to
follow him into the forest. My lashes are caught in my eyes.

We hurry away from the lights and the voices behind us.
I can hear them all breathing. Torch-light lancing through
leaves. Ouma reads the trees like road signs. The soldiers
behind turn into blind corners. Their tongues at work,
shouting orders. Ouma stops and points us to run as he
watches shadows returning to the dark behind enemy
lines. He too has become the night and disappears the way
we came, in search of blood. We keep running towards
Kenya. The undiluted dark reveals nothing but the path
just in front of us. My mother has me on her back now.
From behind, there are screams like a cat crying or a live
chicken being skinned, then silence. We are hemmed in
by the river. Ouma falls out the sky into the path in front.
His raised fist ordering us to stop.

OUMA: Mama, this is as far as I go. I was only able to stop
   two of them. Within the hour there will be twenty soldiers
   in these woods. Take this!

YOUNG NICK: He leads us to the lake where a boat is waiting
   – hidden.

OUMA: You will have to row east. That will take you to Kenya. A thousand long strokes five times will get you there. You will be there by sunrise.

YOUNG NICK: And now we are three. Mama puts me into the boat. The water is calm but it still tips to one side. I gasp. She grabs it and steadies it. I look at Mirembe. Water leaks down her leg. She is crying. She is holding her belly. Her eyes are lightning, staring at Mama.

MAMA NICK: Oh God!

YOUNG NICK: She is crying and crying,

MAMA NICK: Father, help us!

MIREMBE: No no. Shh shh. They will find us.

YOUNG NICK: Mama is crying now. She puts her hand over her own mouth to stop herself from screaming.

MIREMBE: Your son.

YOUNG NICK: The boat has started to drift away slowly from the riverbank. Mama walks into the water. It is up to her knees.

MIREMBE: Go. We will be okay. I promise. We will be okay.

NARRATOR NICK: And then I don't remember. All I could hear is my mother counting to a thousand under her breath.

MAMA NICK: One. Two. Three. Four. Five. Six. Seven. Eight…

//SD: Airplane sounds.

NARRATOR NICK: Back then all I knew was my Father (the sun) and my mother (the moon), both immovable objects of light and heat. Then there is me, the earth, since the age of four spinning on its own axis as well as the orbit of the sun. Gravity has bound my mortal body to this dance. *(Beat.)*

But how do we step outside ourselves into the vastness of space, its peace, its darkness, that nothing can penetrate? *(Beat.)* We just about notice the changing dance of the seasons. Do you notice the moon creeping up on your face without introduction? Only when the earth, moon and sun stand in line for a moment does our world imitate the darkness of the cosmos. The moon creeps along the face of the sun, the antelope stops in panic. All of us that live look up! *(Beat.)*

Will the sky fall down? Will the earth cave in? Only the darkness from which we all were made has the answer. At times like this, when we are closest to our fear, the moon swims away, the sun's heat and light are restored to full power and the earth is as we remember it – as the darkness lifts from us. But not for long.

//SD: Airplane sounds.

SCENE 17

//Projection: Heathrow Airport, November 1979 – Night.

CUSTOMS OFFICER: First day of spring – won't you be needing a coat…?

There are not many of your kind here, you see, so the question is – and be as open as you feel – why are you here?

So you do speak English. Who taught you that then?

Your Father – where is he?

Home – where is home?

Don't stop there. So if your father's there, why are you here?

Is your dad a soldier?

You must miss him. You can't be staying that long then.

You don't know. Pity! You're going to miss Big Ben. Have you met him?

Yes!

He is a clock. Guilty. You are just like one of us. Isn't he, Paul? Your English is better than mine, Nicholas. That is your name?

Strange name for a Ugandan boy. How do you spell that?

With an *ache*.

And this other name, Bwire, what does that mean…? Born in the night!

Right. So tell me more about this journey across the wild with tanks?

I wonder if you could explain how you got to Nairobi with no passport?

Matatu! Is that a fruit? What's that? You have a great imagination.

Admit it: I'll put my cards on the table. You are not
the first boy to travel with a woman, after pointing at a
globe, to the shape of Europe, and fly towards it. It is
easy to invent a past with snakes, rebel leaders, guns,
the end-of-the-world, boy soldier, passengers on the bus,
motionless in the middle of the road, a mountain, a man
who understands your dream. But when you arrive here
with no address or passport and a mother with a different
surname, fighting back her tears. Well it seems, the
question is, whether or not I believe it. Take your place in
line with all of the others.

*//YOUNG NICK has one piece of luggage, one passport. The noise
of an airport comes into focus. The CUSTOMS OFFICER leaves to
talk to his colleague. The light fades on YOUNG NICK in the airport
interrogation room, waiting.*

NARRATOR NICK: I want you to close your eyes…

End.

WWW.OBERONBOOKS.COM

Follow us on Twitter @oberonbooks
& Facebook @OberonBooksLondon